33 1/3

33 1/3
Soap Opera Sonnets

◇◇◇

Barbara Schweitzer

Little Pear Press
Seekonk, MA

Little Pear Press
Seekonk, MA 02771
www.littlepearpress.com
© 2008 by Barbara Schweitzer
Cover photographs by Natalie Gruppuso
Design by Christina Gruppuso
Printed in the USA
ISBN: 0-9746-9113-5
ISBN 13: 978-0-9746-9113-8
Library of Congress Control Number: 2008921954

To Bill and Kay

Contents
Soap Opera Sonnets

Blowfish

She's all windows like an aquarium
full of blowfish who deceive for mere sport;
it takes no stir or scare to puff her up;
her quills – she likes to use mixed metaphor –
are always aquiver, giving her sights
from a distance most don't have, so enmeshed
in the living as they are. While she might
stand close to any or all of them, flesh
warming to her touch, while she blows kisses
like fish their bubbles – such delightful things
tickling and prismatic – while she wouldn't miss
an opportunity to kick back, sing,
the only camaraderie she thinks
she'll survive is like the squid's with its ink.

1

She is known by the minks she keeps

She would never deign to touch a doorknob
leading in to what she would never claim
as squalor, for that would make her a snob
and she would not allow blight on her name,
or his, for he carries her now like silt
in a deep river unaware of weight
inside its strong currents busy tilting
to the light. She would never utter hate
toward a Christian, would turn her rouged cheek,
check any stirring of venial sin,
let her thoughts weep at the opera, seep
through her pores to the inside of her mink;
she's the best of any woman, so *sure,*
pitying all poor souls who can't be her!

Gilbert and…

He claims Sullivan of *Gilbert and…* his
nearest relative in fame. Once he met
an aficionado on a ship
whose rapture at his proximity set
him in his cabin for two weeks, and he
slinked around avoiding her for that time,
succeeding but for once when at lunch she
jumped him from behind and threatened she limned
clear through him, feared witch! For her, he counted
on his fingers the five branches across
generations, him to Sir, then bounded
to his cabin, heaving, quivering, lost.
Smartened since, he still sings his pedigree,
now, like a mikado, *confidently.*

Hetty finally gets a real boyfriend

Someone rifled through his glove compartment
in her driveway. Snow prints led through a yard
over to a porch door. His deportment,
when she said her first no, soft voice turned hard:
she knows now he spoke half-true when he said:
what I have I want for you. He meant not
long marriage but longing, continued dread,
not full heart at ease but stomach in knots,
neighbors on the block, spouse to bed early,
a free-range man, meteor, not a star
held in orbit by rings as on fingers –
he wants those for her? Now he's gone too far:
stalking, parking outside her boyfriend's flat.
Call his wife? Rat on him? Let that be that?

2

Inside inside

Bells spread white sound through the lavender street
to her house two doors down from St. Jude's Church.
Dusk purls her windows, parishioners meet
their raveled breaths as they rush from the curb
and begin prayers before they're even in
the vestibule, prayers of the late: *let there*
be more pews than just the front few open!
She reads, like tea leaves, unrest in the air
perpetuated by misplaced ardor,
she thinks, as her heart yawns to the long day.
A barking dog picks her up, gnaws at her,
drops her in the ravine a block away.
She sighs. Looking out is not being in.
She sips her gin, gleans a bird, oh! a wren.

The seduction in Exeter

The Grey Goose is not dead. It rests its head
in the freezer next to the bluefish, shelved
for greatest effect. She's already led
the young man, twenty (no? less?) past the realm
of questionable responsibility.
He is alarmingly charming and brash
ensnaring everyone at the party
with panache no Baby Boomer can match;
why'd she answer him when he'd asked her where?
Now he swigs it and flirts and, outrageous!
lifts his glass: "I knew Mountain Dew would fare
better with a splash," cocks his head, "To us!"
When she was his age, old men plied her with drink.
Now their age, his fingers wrapping, she can't think.

He's on his way up

Father's ex is a treacherous mother!
He'd leave her too if he could, endlessly
pruning his patience, purpling his other
concerns, saying she'll take away his *keys*?
Home by eight? What's she bustin' *his* chops for?
He plans how to disarm her: band practice
till ten – lying so often now it bores
him. In the field, cheerleaders' pointy tits
cheer him up, that and his appointment, his
assignation with the lady's Ketel One.
She's smitten with him, and why not? RIZ-D
is just months away. When all's said and done
her generous sources of libation
drown out any sort of aggravation.

3

Screw her Nikes

It's not becoming for a girl to walk
so much. Funny how many times such words
began the end, at least three she could talk
about, the last one most dreadful she'd heard,
ever, she thinks, as she picks up her pace
entering the nursing home's familiar
halls. What's wrong? She's young and pretty pretty,
she's a good aide, gets paid good, what's with her
that undoes so many men? Her cousin
thinks her independence is too jarring.
Men are scared of girls so fit. Two dozen
saw fit to leave her. She wonders how far
to go, what the proper mileage might be –
she'd be willing to eschew her Nikes.

Away like a snowbird

The juncos carouse in the snow too much.
Their bottoms show their sins like small harlots
stained by their pleasures; she thinks maybe such
signs in nature mean something but she's got
awful bad at interpreting. She thinks
it's time to go out like D.H. Lawrence
wrote, which novel she forgets, and these finks
might figure her out if she asks them. Hence,
she'll just get one of them to roll her out
past the curve next snowfall. They look away
and she's down the path in her chair, the route
she knows to bittersweet. She'll crawl all day.
Imagine her secret finally gone,
frozen guiltlessly inside her by dawn.

Black dog

Nothing to do, bark a lot, walk a lot,
yellow line down the road, traffic faster
than it used to go, every year more sod
covering up the bare spots where my bladder
always goes off, an irritant, near blind,
I can see better only at night, cars
standing out so bright, no mistaking lights.
Nothing to do, walk, walk, but not too far,
licking logs, smelling a stump, something new
perks up a dog a lot, nuzzle in, bite
a bit, hit bone, teeth hurt to have to chew,
can't do what I used to do, reached my height,
and doggone it, it's finally true: I'm sick.
I forego my shtick of learning new tricks.

4

We never talked to our neighbors

She ran over him with a lawn mower.
You can't get more gruesome than that. Details
don't have to be specific. We owe her
already for an event that won't pale
in the face of most acts. Now she retracts
her intention, but we suspect it's to
save her neck, not sincerely given. Facts
rather clearly show lawn mowers go too
slow to render a self-defense defense
defensible. If she's to save her ass
she'd better confess she lost her senses
long before she went out to cut the grass.
Maybe she'll cop a plea, get on TV –
but lawns'll never be the same on our street.

Two-way street

Marriage is a two-way street. You can go
one way or the other when you learn things
untoward: they'll be wee bumps in the road,
or, the dead end of all that's promising.
I chose the one most traveled by and ran
right over all he said; now he's best dead.
It's funny how your mind tricks, how you can
do what you want to do, being misled
by your thoughts. I thought I wanted to stay
tangled in the grass, get past his affair,
love the afternoon air, make up – but – way
too forgiving, it seems. Blood in his hair
clinched that. Was I trying to hide my crime
by mowing over him? Could be. Seems right.

Her kid's been around the block

Four sticky Cheerios plant round bull's eyes
for her sponge, zip, zip, zap, they're gone, never
to reappear, out the ionosphere right
through gravity which she recently read
has a speed she can't understand since she
thought it was what held her upright on earth
but it bullets like light apparently
which is far faster than sound, (lightning births
thunder), and now, under his bed, he's hid
Playboys, Sports Illustrateds. Where'd he get
these? She sits down to do some comparing
but none of these models had kids. Why fret,
for, as Marilyn Monroe observed wisely,
fast or not, we all get got by gravity.

5

High crime

In this high crime district past the liquor
store, to the market, she walks, shoes untied,
braids in her hair, she could be a poster,
so cute, just a youngster needing a ride.
She steps into the market, and you dread
the evening news with the gang, the mistake,
shuffling, a stray bullet, on the floor dead
like Red Riding Hood eaten alive – wait!
She emerges, gallon milk in her hand.
You're glad! – Then, the picture of her mother
nodding off on heroin, contraband
hid in the youngest's diaper, the other
kids starving but for this parentified
child. Skipping? to the car? her mother? smiles?

About that thumping

There is that thumping every night, sidled
passings in the vestibule. He's handsome
but you won't let him catch your eye, and why?
Because you're a prude! They're married! Can't some
people have sex without embarrassment?
How enlightened do you think you are? You're
smoldering over their joys? It's not thin
walls, steady rhythm or that you need more
sleep. It's that you're not getting your own thumps!
"How's it going, neighbor," he asks one day
in the elevator. "You like these plump
babies?" He coddles fat tomatoes. "Say,
why not come up for some antipasto?
Our head-banging son wants to say hello."

Characters' assassin wanted

Lofty intentions do not novels make
nor ideas that don't carry a plot
nor meanderings that have lots of sex; rakes
can be the garden variety; not
a lot of first novels ever get sold;
nobody knows but that one great writer
who didn't succeed until she was quite old,
the age and the name always eluding her,
though she's been told the story untold times.
This hottest January of record,
she brought only wools and not enough limes
for the Lime Rickeys that keep her sane; she's bored,
and the whole winter in this urban loft
is her prize for what she can't finish off.

6

The bachelor on the block

Just as the goldfinches were getting back
their color at the end of a ceaseless
winter, before he saw a robin, stacks
of cordwood halfway down, before the lease
was up on his Corvette and his ex had
not yet moved out on him, but did that spring
when his promotion became lateral
permanently, he took up exercising
to ease his mind; just when open windows
came in and before air conditioning
rendered what he heard whirs of condensers,
he listened to families yell, motioning
him in a direction of bachelorhood
that ran much further than he ever would.

Stray cat

Like a fluff of buff, she came to the door,
mute, scruffy; no welcome mat underfoot,
she curled there like one of those brittle gourds
still rustling in November air. It shook
him out of his old doldrums; he even
bought some chocolates with Kit 'N Kaboodles
that he let the cat sniff when she'd eaten
her food from her dish, but Pad Thai noodles
ended up her favorite treat. He got
her take-out Thursdays. How satisfying
when she purred, so seemingly happy! Not
that he was into anthropomorphizing.
The hermetic type, he didn't even like
that the human types could bring him a smile.

Think she'll go eat worms

It was a surprising pickle she found
herself in, not what she thought would happen
when she told her husband (and took the ground
right out from under him) that his son, when
she calculated carefully, couldn't be
his. She didn't think she'd be in such a jam
when he moved out, plaintively begging he
be credited the progeny. Her damn
neighbor couldn't cut the mustard, deigned to stay
with the pasty wife he claimed for ten years
he wanted to leave, what a sleaze, but, hey,
either way, pumpernickel or rye, here, here!
she'll raise her glass to all the years when, who
ever knew? she'd had her cake and ate it too.

7

Across from the park

Sunday mornings are the best, the whole heft
of day hers when she waves the truck at the curb
away, half-crumpled still; that's why she left.
He never did nothing on time but urge
her to trust him once, the one and only
time she shouldn't've. She's heard fertility
has a weird narrow window; how he squeezed
through hers is no joke! Never mind though, she's
free the livelong day, until seven, eight
the latest; the little one back then, wet,
neglected, but at least, for now, not weight
around her neck. She cinches her robe, lets
motherhood drop, plops on a white plastic
chair. She'll kick back, do nothing, not a lick!

Merry-go-round

A tiger crawls up and around his arm,
studs glitter his belt, he wears leather pants
and boots; he rocks. He's a full five-alarm
for the girl who comes on Sundays; by chance
she'll get there late enough for him to close
the booth and hang with her, he's got some dope
he bets she'll like; up-down, the horses go,
the clown song he likes plays, it's a tad slow
today. He hopes she'll come, he knows a way
to the monkey cage; a kid is crying.
It makes him nervous the dad makes him stay
when the kid obviously hates the ride.
You shouldn't never make a kid cry for fun.
Merry-go-rounds ain't made for everyone.

Taking her Sunday licks

To her there's hardly enough air, silver
plane slivering the sky; she's dizzy, high,
incomplete still, another two; will her
lungs give out before her legs do? Oh why
suffer so? Ahead the calliope
jingles the air and people hum as if
tuning themselves for a song, but here she
imprisons herself in iron-fisted fartleks.
In the distance sugar shivers in sheets
across the street undoing the youngster
whose cotton candy gets torn up by weak
gusts forewarning rain. That sure won't stop her.
Like the mailman from his appointed task,
it's marathon or bust, and why? Don't ask.

8

Studying to be an entrepreneur

She would scream but it would do no good; he
made his bed and now lies in it alone
three hours by car away from her. While he
wigs out about her absence on the phone,
she holds it at arm's length like all she does,
cutting corners, cutting hair, cutting class
to get by, heart squeezed as in latex gloves.
She's scissored him down, and you bet your ass
he'll marry her by June, for she hears cracks
in his tune now she's away. He won't shirk
from her sharkskin skirt and her tricks that track
him down like smart bombs hitting where it hurts.
As he pines for his missing *Valentine,*
she relaxes, permanent in his mind.

Studying religious right

Must be Tuesday again, for there's the sign
like an omen, asterisk on his week,
the red Mercedes, profligate icon
taking two parking places on the street.
Today is snow, so sure enough, she's furred
clear down to her ankles, how disgusting
it is – such casual disregard, murder
of minks, of street signs, her stinking luster
re-sculpted, massaged by servants of sin,
packed up and repackaged again. He'll not
watch her leave, that's what he'll do, he'll begin
Ezekiel, stop stalking the salon.
Soon, if everything works out right, he'll opt
to right that misnamed blight, that beauty shop.

Studying to be an entrepreneur 2

A stir announces the jay's arrival;
juncos, sparrows, chickadees promptly bleed
into green limbs while their gray-blue rival
claims its purchase with admirable greed,
he thinks, fiddling with the screen when a gust
of wind whistles in, and he can't abide
drafts when he studies (because he's rusty
as Detroit); martinis with friends last night
didn't cotton him to the task; he wishes
he were somewhere else, facing Saharan
sands; dry rot has invaded his mind. This
town blows! He drifts … yep, his course is errant,
calls home: "I quit school to follow my dream."
He has a game plan, a pyramid scheme!

9

Woman trying to smell the primroses

No flower pot could get by unsmelled, she
fervently desires the scent of primrose,
but all the Stop and Shop kind are mixed breeds,
hybrids, the colorful kind that lack those
special pheromones that brightened her heart
each breath. This year none carry delicate
earth in their petals; it's not a good start
for a mournless heart, must be profligate
prophecy here amidst supermarket
greenery, predicting she'll never be
free of irascible memory that harks
back to effervescent mornings when he
used flowers to vaporize her defense,
to convince her love wasn't evanescent.

The Marlboro woman

Flank steak, chuck ground meat, chicken thighs on sale,
Wonder Bread, jam, peanut butter – super
chunky? No, smooth. She can see them inhale
a nut, Heimlich, the emergency room!
The thought upsets the whole condiment aisle.
Spaghetti, ramen, four packs, a quarter
each – great! – chicken soup; the kids're quiet
in the fake red car, steering under her
half-filled cart, stomach a knot, eggs, whole milk,
cheapest o-j from concentrate, she'll skip
by the Popsicles, a bit guiltily,
so she lets them get cookies, bites her lip,
adds up, makes sure she calculated right.
She needs a carton of Marlboro Light.

A spill on aisle seven

He stacks up the pounds of flesh, T-bone steaks,
a dozen, frozen French fries, case of Cokes,
the fixings for his poker friends; it makes
him feel alive having the guys over
after the honeymoon in Hawaii.
He'll pick up booze on the way home, beer, wine;
he grabs some flowers to give her; she'll see
how glad he is she egged him on. In line,
he gives her a call, just a love's quickie
with hopes she won't leave till he's there, but she
isn't home and won't answer her cell; he
feels his stomach churn; they've not had any
dinners apart since she walked down the aisle
of his heart. She made him do this, now *why*?

10

Found religion

They shared their secrets when it was too late.
One of them drank herself to bankruptcy.
One of them drank herself to spite and hate.
And one is still drinking herself silly.
The oldest reigns over the debacle
with the same fear in his jaw he acquired
from the Ohioan corn fields, cruelly held
by his ankles at their edge, having heard
stories of monsters that stirred the waving
green arms about to swarm over his head
unless he begged them just right, and they saved
him from the maw of the corn fiends. The dread
he held didn't turn him into a drinker
but into a religious non-thinker.

Barn raising

Had calves died on him before, nothing new,
fierce bellies wasting the feed; you mashed it,
hand-cupped it into the mouths, but you knew
when the corn brew didn't stop but whipped through it
like you're pouring in one end just to watch
it pour out the other, you knew, it's not meant
to live, and the grandson might as well catch
how that works now better than later, can't
coddle boys; he won't get no 4-H prize
this spring. Still, losing his yellowed thumbnail
under soft fur, round ear, he thinks what size
grief do you allow? The poor calf will die
in hunger and feed. Only we perceive
the interminable pain in between.

Consciousness razing

She took so many years to grow into
herself that by the time she did, her life
had rent the seams; in despair she turned to
her past (less her indiscretions) to find
what to do. She preferred remembering
tender spots like the cat who gnawed corn husks,
so she didn't get far, sentiment limiting
the whole truth that is much more like Russian
Roulette than Hallmark. Still the metaphor
of the cat with its husks gave her solace
in her penned-in consciousness, for before
she had that cat, it had picked garbage; thus,
she thought, no matter what goods we incur,
we never escape what we first prefer.

11

Being neighborly

The front porch sags toward the sidewalk. Neighbor
goes ahead and shovels, nagged by guilty
conscience for all the years he didn't, a hoard
of kids underfoot and dogs yapping. She
needs concrete help now to bolster the rot
set in, but can't do nothing about that
till spring thaws the ice. She's awful nice, not
that he hadn't liked her through the years, what
with her cheery smile, pastel uniforms,
every night at five gathering the kids round,
widening more and more each year, her poor
knees took a beating, but didn't knock her down.
Through the window, hair's grown back on her head,
she waves hello from her hospital bed.

True value

Eighty acres, divided it by three,
soon's he took five for himself, the market
too good to let this generation be
locked in sentimentality. Farther
along his mansion got, the better his
investment shone on the horizon: Mack
trucks, roads rose from former fields; he listened
to giant boulders dynamited, blasts
bellowing clear to the True Value store;
he loved no sound more; and when he is gone,
his name'll live on the strip mall. He adored
these lavish new developments, and none
more than his neighbors' unanimous pleas.
Their effrontery abetted his glee.

You can go home again

Finally this old town is getting cleaned up,
spruced up, even with a new Kohl's – not new down
south, but here? They still think bottled ketchup's
enough modernity. Down on her town
she comes around only when a new job
gives her space or her parents beg her to
have mercy before she goes hobnobbing,
leaving them again for China, Peru,
never little Rhody. There at the head
of the table, the dad's not changed a mite,
the dustless corners welcome sun, the beds
love clean sheets, and Mother still joins the fight
to keep acreage requirements going,
to keep riffraff out and littleness growing.

12

Circus polka

Balanchine an ale? Egads! For the sake
of dance, she holds her response close to her
like Cleopatra's asp; ridicule snakes
through her tongue; she unhisses it, wonders
how long she has to serenade like this,
picking pockets. He laughs at his own jokes,
saving her guile; she can't let down a bit,
must stay on her toes, his family half-owned
this state once; her theme and variation
must be pure, engage him in love of jewels,
in a pas de deux of adoration.
He must add to her rations. By George, she'll
do all for donations, skip to the loo,
choreograph elephants, if she has to.

Demosthenes unbound

If the Phoenix rose from ashes without
shame, soaring on a line of his own wind
should not trouble him. Here, being touted
nationwide as wise, people clamoring
to be at his side, cocktails raised, all fair.
He didn't choose what would become news, headlines
in the New York Times. It was really mere
practice at the mirror, knotting his tie,
gathering words – generally attorneys
are allowed that, no? Now they're toasting him
for what he said when what he meant truly
was sympathy, not gain from the victims.
He now suffers catholic guilt, so condemned,
he'll rise like cream in what they say of him.

Cash cows

He's glad to see the dairy industry
well-represented here, all of them tied
to the governor by a money tree
shading his campaign, and there, riding high
on the crème de la crème is the girlfriend
of his friend kowtowing to an unslim
contributor; all a lot of corn-fed
baloney, glue for the few. Lucky him,
he's one of them, tips his glass till the last
cow comes home, then rearranges his pitch,
counts up the cash that will bank the next bash.
It's lots of moolah, but fêtes with the rich
can be all-consuming. Satin and silk,
back-patting, putting on the front. Got milk?

13

Choosing shoes

Her pigskin purse no longer pleases her,
its clasp oafish, out of style. It lasted
a good while longer than Prada, preferred
until her loose change, loosed in the attached
coin purse, rattled her. The green Coach: gauche. She
hates Ann Klein. She'll stalk the mall tomorrow
or the city next week, but suddenly
all her purses are just sacks of sorrow.
Shopping makes her life seem awfully long.
She shuts the closet, feels tagged like in those
games of chase. "You're it," they would taunt, the song
slung over their shoulders. You're it alone.
She'd be so much happier as a shoe,
companioned with matching purse, always two.

The former pig farmer

Mountains of tires could burn for decades,
he supposes, but once he saw trash heaps
turned into parks where none worried which way
the wind blew or what sparks were loose, but he's
sure the town council will oppose his plan
to plant over smolder; they'd rather hang him
like that blue jay tangled in netting back
of his garden, its feathers collapsing
its hollowed chest. They'd like *him* in a net
on the Common, people throwing garbage
at him, he bets. Hey, the *EPA* let
him be. Why can't they? This offal seepage
in the bay isn't their care. They're simply
incensed by the stench. It's olfactory.

A stitch in time

The Johnny-jump-ups carpet the side yard.
She filled the bird feeder twice, the thistle
bringing yellow finches; it isn't hard
to see summer summoning wolf whistle
days. She stops, mid-stitch, thinks, did her husband
fix the bird bath, cracked in two? She's making
a quilt for the baby born with no hands
down the street, a young couple mistaking
youth for safety, but who wouldn't? In her day
amnio didn't exist; if it did, she'd
not have had it – it went against her faith,
though she can't say for sure. She's glad the weeds
in her yard are killed after the spring thaws.
It's nice pesticides get rid of them all.

14

Parsimony's wife

He is more skilled than Demosthenes, seed
in his beak, tongued clean in a second, red
bright on the windowsill she filled with feed
an hour ago; her husband will be fed
up again with her frivolity. He's
warned her not to waste money on birds … so
she memorizes the cardinal's worries,
how he can't focus on pleasure or know
safety's embrace or how easy it is
to lose one's self in the grace of mornings.
His life is one elongated fear, chicks
mincing it from their parents' adoring
regurgitations, not too unlike her –
a wife who must be careful with her words.

Serotonin reuptake un-inhibited

Blimey fartface! and *frig you, too! Up yours!*
Don't even *think* about it! Driving, cupped
phone at ear, zipping up 95, perked
alert, her pharmaceutical stock up,
and she's dipped in her samples for the docs.
Today it's down Fenway to the Mass Ave.
practice, Doc Cutie Pie to lunch! This job
rocks! Everywhere there's pure profit to have
and to hold, and she's grasping it as fast
as she can; twenty-six, thin, slick, pretty
as sin, her sales figures have them aghast
at her sass. She's on her way up and whee!
She only hopes the U.S. won't recede
from its commitment to corporate greed!

What's in a name

Bovine black-white clearly demarcated
in the rock-riddled field, sere grass, a brook
winkling out the middle where mud-sated
beasts straddle earth and ephemeral, looking
all the more flummoxed when she calls their names.
Every day for twelve years, she strode by them
placidly grazing; it has been the same
for twelve years each day but now ... rumblings, dim
shifts in her body, edges reworking,
grayed ends unraveling, and through her center
not gentle or mild, a crater's murky
stirring grows shadows, catapulting her
deep into caverns of medicine's shame:
pale, face to face with its terrible names.

15

A good night's rest

In the mayor's office behind the scenes, they
laugh at his gaff, though it's not laughable,
since they will take the heated calls all day
from constituents; the irascible
center of the maelstrom won't. They watched him
fire his aides, but they'll weather this, union-
safe, phew! Thank public service collectives
everywhere for how they give permission
to breathe easier in reality
of electoral stupidity that
eventually leaves them alone to clean.
They'll sit through all the meetings to be sat.
Unlike reporters, their sleep won't be robbed.
They'll sleep in peace in bed, not on their jobs.

Rest stop

It took a well-placed phone call demanding
change at the former ski slope, denuded
by the southern clime climbing north, blanding
seasons, one to the other. Polluted
highway rest stops can't be tolerated
by town people who are so upstanding,
church-going, suburban, inundated
with outsiders who love the place. Planning
committees on how to serve housing needs
took time out of their agendas to solve
the problem, which was – put elegantly –
too many bushes at the sylvan stop
causing hanky-panky that is too much
with which a good citizen can put up.

Keep the riffraff with the rest

Her father's turning over in his grave.
She could feel his shuddering through her sleeves.
Utterly preposterous that he gave
that corner stretch of land to have it seed
a stupid plan environmentalists
conceive! A bike path that will wind through her
neighborhood? She's not heard of anything
so out of sync with the needs of the world!
Her family gives to the church, volunteers
in soup kitchens, at the hospital desk,
even helps the neediest. She's no mere
establishmentarian! Her dad's death
won't be used like this. She'll sure knock on doors,
petition for a reroute down two blocks more.

16

Going to war

One just had to steel one's self to these things,
learning how to be seaworthy, of course,
but it's hard to understand how God wrings
out each deployment day to the same coarse
gray, no separation from sky and sea
and ship. The enlisted men and their wives
at the docks, all grim in goodbyes – maybe
all that grief affects the skies. He arrived
at oh-six-hundred, lined the officers
up for prayers to start the mission. This year
it is more serious than most, they're sure
to see combat, though where? It's not yet clear.
At the twenty-year mark his thoughts on war
endured a sea change, but thoughts stay ashore.

At peace in the dale

Navy guys used to rent houses in town.
It was wild then. Girls had variety,
quite a few broken promises, too. Down
under, we still miss them, though property
values have risen; that's the economy,
not because we're rid of them. She had liked
one of them once and too ferociously –
still thinks of him every summer. They hiked
from his backyard down to the park when his
wife visited her sick mom; wow! never
got such good loving as there on those swings –
her therapist says it wasn't love, never!
mere fun – making an officer *gentleman*
turn base. Maybe? Still, she wished he'd bought land.

Civil service

They still call him Admiral everywhere.
Understandably. His changed career
has hardly moved his position a hair.
He's still the center of his universe,
obeyed, and everyone benefited
from his retirement. He gets to build
his new business where he elicited
most of his contracts from his old-but-still-
useful contacts. And, admired for more
than his commanding manners, he does lots
for art and children, has an open door
policy for charity, sponsors non-
controversial things. Not for money,
he sets up shop. For magnanimity.

17

Weather predilections

From Woonsocket to Westerly, R-I,
weather is a topic addressed dearly
as one does a lover who acts unwise,
testing wind with wayward thumb, severely
hampering chances of fair skies ahead,
in other words, ceaselessly – like her search
for *the one*, pursuing him like the Red
Baron kamikazing every bar, thirst
wreaking confusion, strewing thunderstorms
of elbows and limbs, dance floors of danger
and the unsavory aftermaths, warm
wet and earthy, but needing wider range.
She goes after him like the thunderbolt
and, ever the fair-weather friend, with hope.

Driving habits

Next block over it happened on Tuesday.
Lady in a habit of backing up
without looking, in a hurry. The way
I heard, he didn't know what hit him, ruptured
three discs, broke his knees, both of them, before
he realized the muffler was over him,
then, his life passed before his eyes – and more!
the chassis, too. But he doesn't blame them.
His career was changed then. No U-P-S
and the nice brown uniform; it's patterns
now. The johnnies with open backs are less
trouble than pajamas. The sweet intern,
half his age, says he'll walk again someday
though he should stay away from the driveways.

It's a sign

In the vee of the C-V-S sign down
the hill past Bev's Place and the road over
where the River Furniture Store went out
of business fifteen or so years ago,
the pharmacy where Ma worked afternoons
when Dad got laid off and he collected
that time and Ma never knew we skipped school
because she panicked when he elected
to be a jerk and never work again,
at that place, in the vee, you won't believe
there's a nest and pestering baby wrens
crowded in it, open-mouthed, and you see
how nice birds can be: *both* their mom and dad
are frenzied, feeding their babies like mad.

18

Oblivion in the works

He never slows for the elements, swerves
around the plow, the white sheet of his wake
starting her at the window, unnerving
her to begin the day. For goodness sakes,
he could have waited to turn the corner
to drive so crazy. Hazy circles steam
her breath, the only evidence of her
that would form today; with Herculean
effort she might get dressed, but why be brave
in the face of solitude? Mired inside
the snow, nobody will know if she behaves.
He, in his SUV, will love the ride
through the blizzard to the hospital rounds
while she, invisible for days, stays snowbound.

Mourning

He remembers when brokenness became
true for his little girl, but for him, when?
Now the new bird feeder must be replaced,
ungrateful squirrels ceaselessly bending
wires – squirrel-proof, ha! – away from the tray
until the seeds aren't contained. They've bitten
the hand that feeds them again. Sorely quaint
that they repeat their rank behavior when
he longs for a place that might stay wholly
whole, the place to believe in the way she
believed in heaven years ago, fully
enshrouded with hope, the child mournfully
crying, "It's broken! Broken!" at the sky,
the crescented moon lying in her eye.

Where does nature get off

The receiving blanket his mother made
is too loud for baby swaddle, but she'd
never say such unbehaved words; she'll stay
in the back seat where his haircut needles
her. She mourns the kind of softness between
them she knows they've lost today. He chats on,
polite, never swerving or churning. He
has everything just right, like his hair, done
with precise geometry. Her heart hurts
at the straight line and all the sharpnesses
of the world. The wee fist of a face flirts
briefly but then clouds lose their addresses
overhead unhinging shafts of sunlight.
Poor baby, beginning to train for life.

19

Reese's pieces of her mind

Spoon in her dish, she thinks he was just a
Fig Newton of her imagination.
She says it out loud, *Fig Newton,* afraid
she'll forget the funny phrase. Damnation!
It feels good to slather her mind with smart
talk after such starvation of thought. He's
more insipid than a dish of Walmart's
vanilla, as empty as a Reese's
cup minus the peanut butter. She streams
a mountain of whipped cream atop the mound
of pistachio; how could she have dreamed
such a clunker was her dream man? She's bound
to do better next time. First: on the top
of the requirements will be: a job!

Bad cat

She's shred the popcorn packing everywhere.
She's made a tree of the piano legs,
chased the other cat up and down the stairs
thirteen times for bad luck, chewed the letter
I off the laptop. It lies like a pat
of butter on the carpet, a little
frayed now around the edges. She's been bad,
knows the word, has heard it in the middle
of the dark when she's spread across the bed
tucked between the logs of warm bodies from
wherever luxury's born; she's been fed
plenty good but wants the live birds who hum
in wild keys. Why shouldn't she tear through the house,
kept from real action like thunder from sound!

Snack time

Kit Kat? he'd ask if he didn't mind risking
life and a break from the woman he'd asked
to live her life as his wife; best nixing
politeness, take a bite behind her back.
Does he mind these hours of indecision
at the flatware displays? Some things he knows
without being told: it's best chewing on
a candy bar than offering your choice,
or worst still, running off at the mouth with
some Ikea ideology like:
life's just a half dozen of one or six
of the other. He'll sure swallow that tripe!
Later he'll slip her half of his candy.
She'll be famished from the goods and plenty.

20

Lock her up

She's still recovering from a bad haircut,
slowly, painstakingly working her way
back into life. God knows she's had bad luck
with hairdressers, how many she won't say,
her predilection for danger never
changing. Each time she's delivered deadly
blows to self esteem and follicles, her
resolve to find a permanent home sweeps
through her. She surveys those who happily
keep regular appointments and their coiffed
confidence she wants herself, but then she
forgets when the sheer horror of her doffed
hair recedes by its growing. She still mocks
how her psyche gets lopped off with her locks.

Lock steps

Tangles of dammit vine and bittersweet
measure the fate of great ideas gone
before they rise. A lady's-slipper meets
Indian pipes, mockingbirds flit and hone
their borrowed songs, brush buries the pale path
to the abandoned pit where mules and men
slavishly committed their hours, the math
of their canal now rich, swaddled in green
forgiveness, spring's gift. Lovers traipse there, locked
in turgid embraces; foolhardiness
of a century ago meets their own. Flocks
dispersed since autumn leave behind their nests.
Far from public space, nature has a way
of stealing grand plans to plant love segues.

A lox in time

Lox and cream cheese, bagels, and how to eat
were for her the best part of the "Naming."
Of course, in the synagogue, the freedom
of the children to wander and the range
of voices made her think for some minutes
she might convert, but only if he gives
the religious instruction; she's kidding!
He knows, laughs, Adam's apple aquiver.
His wife, the professor, on the sofa,
stout friends on either side – anorexic!
she's certain of that, and really so full
of rhetoric, where's room for food? She's sick
to know he chooses his wife over her.
These ceremonies exist to deter.

21

Did they really exist

At the bar with the man who would destroy
her life for a little while, she studies
his friend on the other side of him; coy,
fast at gathering facts from a face, she
reads the lies around his mouth, the slivered
dampness in the creases of his down-turned
lips, his eyes, hungry as a bird's, tip her
off, and she wonders how her lover burns
in envy for his conquests when she knows
he has none but his fear of lies, and too:
how could this man not yet known as her foe
want to screw the night away with all whom
his friend imagines; such sad fixations
that even she ignores the translations.

The conquest of neatness

He turns his mattress each time he changes
his sheets, places his glasses carefully
in their case each time he rearranges
his location; he calculates when he
needs to rotate his tires and takes time off
work in order to do so. Clothes are hung
by color and length, all his pants in rough-
equivalent-to-color groups. It stung
him when she refused to share his passion
for order; he could not endure messes
nor accept her frantic explanations
for them. He tried dividing, confesses
he stopped caring for her. Now that she's gone
he's conquered his last fear: being alone.

Misguided

At no point in the morning sunrise could
she put her finger on the trail of dark
and say, here! this is where light joined in; would
she have a meter for such things, she'd mark
null at the place it registered to fool
the inventor of the machine; that's how
she rebelled – in small ways – scoffing all who
make regulations, demarcations, dowels
that measure or bind. Her husband outside
is blocking with string where the sidewalk will
bring friends through his new foyer. She'll still ride
to the front door and track in all the swill
he's willing out. It's hard fighting reason.
She does so only to be displeasing.

22

Best friends 1

He and his chums flung horseshit in the streets
of Cerbere; the town was pleased he left for
Palamos and didn't return for sixteen
years when he and his current paramour
fooled his wife for a Paris conference
then traveled his memories instead of
attending the plush polyglot, the dense
language juggernaut. This woman in love
with this man could see no foreign landscape;
her eyes, her ears, filled with his razzmatazz,
so dazzled for years, she hardly could gaze
at glade, or anything that grazed, for, as
plants grow steady toward artificial light,
she slanted to his words, best friends of lies.

Best friends 2

When her best friend confesses she slept with him,
she registers nothing but feels compelled
to comfort her – oxymoronic twist
like *best friend who sleeps with your lover* – hell!
She has to focus on some other thought,
thank her mind for preventing homicide!
though it flits through, and she knows she ought not
to scream and call her slut! What overrides
the vicious commands is the *curious*.
Studying her friend's physiology, she
posits how they *did it*. This furious
imagining makes her laugh. How did he
so deftly cleft? But that was his true gift.
Even now, he couldn't leave without this rift.

Best friends 3

They buried her mom in a shallow grave,
a cup of her ashes wrapped in a sleeve
of her best blouse, tied with velvet, all saved
from pieces of her clothes. It's hard to grieve
a life so hard to put your finger on.
She focused on the grave-tender's tender
care as he took the shimmering white cloth,
laid it in the rusty hole. To inter
her here made her seem more solid than she'd
ever been; at least she would remember
the scene: sere grass, wounded earth, scattered weeds
and a workman's hands – not a trace of her
mom's sixty years' best friend, though they *had* thought
of burying her in a Lucky Strike box.

23

Higher authority 1

Seeking a higher cause for her despair,
she dismissed her therapist whose theory
that if she broke her isolation, fair
weather would prevail eventually,
infuriated her. How could misery
like hers be reduced to concupiscence!
It'd been years since it rained, besides which, she'd
never liked the deluge; whenever drenched
in sex, she resented it, like a ride
across the Styx. Done with that therapist
missing the shtick of her life! Why'd she hide
her deepest desires? It's hard to admit
that pleasures of connection are so few,
the only one who satisfies is you.

Higher authority 2

If you follow a leaf down from an oak,
aged giant, harboring no ill despite
our mistreatments, if you watch the leaf float
on invisible currents, the air's wile
twisting, willful; if you discern the path
however ragged it might be, the eye
can absorb myriad mirrors scattered
on it, reflecting camaraderie,
even with a tree, if up close enough,
if you stare close enough, and the river
too, and the sea and the gull and on up
the phyla to the man who shucks oysters
at the shore; he's wearing a pink hat, smiles,
rich in the store of replicating life.

Higher authority 3

The mills closed out long ago and went south
where cheap electric and sweet tea abound.
It seemed a cozy arrangement, but now
that cheaper quarters beckon, it's around
and around we go, this ole globe finite
though imaginings aren't. Rocketing off
the Antarctic is the next plan, that ice
just a chip off the capitalist's block!
Most people have to think in narrow terms.
Businessmen break through that strict tyranny,
break the rules to break new ground *forever*!
He's proud to be a part, you betcha-ree-
Bob! He's worked dang hard to get to the top.
He'll fly a hired spaceship before he'll stop!

24

Real estate

She is well-trained in serendipity
silenced to suffer unmet needs in ways
no child can remember, childhood being
blind and amnesiac like wind to waves.
Innocent to upheavals, she describes
her life as a kumquat, not lush, citrus
and small, not noting commotion inside,
how it might rise up in a blaze, a *fuss*
she called it, over just itty details:
a maid's oversight, a car's slow speed, gray
days. Large lives draw her in and like a snail
encased in pretty shell, she moves in haze,
short-sighted by hunger she doesn't know,
moving up to bigger houses to grow.

Real property

She sees exhaustion crawl like a serpent
from ankle up to tight thigh, elastic
against the weight of the object he rent
from Saddam's palace. His sinewy neck
sweats so he glistens in the video
broadcast throughout the whole world, even here
where the oriental from Morocco
accents the kohl of her walls, and the fear
of violence locks her to CNN.
She doesn't know if the man is tired,
if his dusty feet swell under the strain;
hers do in sympathy. Sipping her wine
she waits for a call. On a buying trip,
her husband lets her pick duty-free gifts.

Real headache

This smile was reserved for Sundays after
the Saturday night fevers broke at dawn,
but as she walked the neighborhood with her
greyhound, Dewey, it didn't phase her who saw
through her face to the nothing-prim-about-
her. Librarians are an open book,
ha-ha, on Sunday nights, too. She was out
of sick time so she'll have to take a look
at how long ecstasy can last when you've
got a headache at the reference desk.
She'll probably be grouchy and two of
the student aides irritate her, a risk
of explosion she hopes will pass by noon.
For now, last night still sends her to the moon.

25

In the elevator

He's the new dermatologist in town,
riding the elevator to nineteen
where scads of people wait in paper gowns
for his expert opinion. He will glean
all sorts of scabrous scab and waxy wart,
roseola, and who knows what else; he's
on duty for the walk-ins; his cohorts-
in-skin divvy up the jobs, and the least
fond tasks belong to him, seniority
rules. He tucks in his tie, lifts his chin, twists
his pass key idly; he's parked his new *Z*
in the doctors' lot, happy now to skim
the surface of things for a dozen years.
Getting-in takes your youth, once-in, your fears.

At the river's edge

She found a little path from the clinic
to the river's edge where she saw five swans
arguing like the nurses on her shift.
She wished she could read the swans' lexicon
to see how they all managed to let go
and float together in the strong currents.
One of them seemed the least senior, knowing
to glide on the sidelines with neck more bent,
less essed – yet he didn't drift away too far
or drift in too close – that seemed the secret.
Still, unless you're a porcupine, you are
unable, it seems, to decline to get
your feet wet. Even skimming the surface
as she does, people get through to hurt you.

In the car

The doc would take six clumps and blood might come
when he eliminated anything –
but he should have no pain, or maybe some.
The greatest he knew would be explaining
to his wife who refused to believe he
could fall for medicine's antics. She scoffed
at these new blood tests looking bad when we
were just fine on the surface. She loved what
she believed in! Lots more than she loved him.
It had been years living in abstinence.
Going to the biopsy alone didn't
phase him; he wouldn't notice her absence.
He just hoped he wouldn't keel over in fright.
It'd be embarrassing if he couldn't drive.

26

Fowl traffic

No one in front knew such a fat bird flew,
so they slowed as he crossed low to the road.
Agawk! Not a hawk or an owl, all too
small, though hued the same. Someone must have known
its name, but by that time the traffic stopped –
all motley-colored SUV's and cars
lined up like so many starlings who drop
on a wire to pearl the horizon – snarled
and all dandered-up, banty-roostered mad,
he only checked his watch, blamed some turkey
for the jam, and indeed! that's what had had
everybody's eyes lifted loftily
as it flew across 95 – barely!
He'd never believe *fowl*. Just cursed foully.

Water fires

He was always sending her *bons baisers*
in the mornings on the silver platter
of his subject lines, little reminders
of what she was missing by being her
own worst enemy, or so he said, led
on by morals she didn't really have if
she really meant what she said when she said
she loved him. He treated her like plaintiff
to his defense of his own knots, married
too long to leave, he argued, but she could!
and then they would wander through the city
traffic, anonymous, reek of burned wood
from the braziers firing the river
in hot kisses like his words flaring hers.

Providence

Their move to the suburbs was subversive,
two dynamos in traffic like Joe Schmoes
each day – they didn't plan the fun would outlive
the first few months when even the peep toads
made them slightly dizzy, and the pleating
and unpleating accordion traffic
squeezed days to goings-and-returns, but see,
their house and yard and white fence made addicts
out of them. Soon her girth changed, made commutes
singular, the swing set progenitor
of wobbly glee and a spring bruise or two.
They gambled in futures, but their front door
reached apogee of all they thought they'd be,
and they drove to and fro so happily.

27

Careful

He calls when the switchboard operator's
left for the day, pleased to know her cell phone
number by heart; she couldn't call anymore
for emergencies – like if her plane won't
leave on time, she forgot the cash he got,
if she changed her mind or lost her ticket
or some other disaster he allots
this trip; his imagination flies jet-
speed to all exigencies she might meet
so, easiest just to give her a call
and put his feverish mind at ease.
She tries to calm him down once and for all:
you worry overtime, you knucklehead!
Save your overtime for your work instead!

Carefree

She's hunting for shoes in LA's Marshall's.
One foot in front of the other, she walked
the ten or so blocks in old Aerosoles,
the only soul on foot on the sidewalks.
She's on vacation so nothing matters.
She can wander streets or aisles aimlessly,
stay in, watch bad TV, do what for her
is rest for its lack of depth, perfectly
fitting for this Hollywood trip. She finds
a mismatched shoe in her size, seeks its mate.
The soft accent of the shoe clerk seems kind;
not much here is unpleasant. One could sate
one's self on this mindlessness – ah, the shoe! –
now what will she do in an hour or two?

Careless

She lost her footing a few years ago.
He noticed it by scent, someone else's,
or maybe by base instinct, he wouldn't know,
but fought inside to avoid the battle.
She had wanted to be carefree, footloose,
but was just careless. He ignored the signs:
the calls, the loose-leaf pad under the goose-
necked lamp with the other's name, meeting times,
each inviting him to grind underfoot
her corruption, but he'd have none of it.
Cataclysm not his rhythm, he'd put
up with her adultery, a tactic
not unlike the stealth of photosynthesis,
letting light digress into a leaf, shift.

28

Scraping by

She said flutists were a dime a dozen,
if you want a future in orchestra
you should play the bass, even violins
are no good, the harp is a fine oeuvre
in the right city. Barely scraping by
takes her breath away, and now her mother
reminds her of her mistakes, how awry
she has always gone, the stubborn other
of her mind the culprit. Apparently
oppositional was her position
throughout daughterhood, she deserved to see
chickens come home to roost; look what she'd done!
She'd failed so badly now, she knew she had
accomplished that which made her mother glad!

Scraping paint

He could taste the black heat rising, asphalt-
borne, stirred as the sun stun-blasted noon; soon
he'd break for lunch, the thought catapulted
him through the next minutes of scraping, through
the grimace of his boss as he climbed down
the ladder to the patch of scraggly brush
in the yard of the tenement around
which his painting job would revolve. This much
was certain: six week's pay for aching pounds
of flesh. A mockingbird flicked his tail, flew
to the roof and sang a titmouse's song.
A little thief, he thought, but then, he knew
the kind of freedom such sweet lying wrought.
He could croon like that, too, and did, a lot.

Scraping together

No Habitat for Humanity here,
no Nobel Prize winner in his bosses,
no creative extracurricular
credits to be had, too bad! It's a loss
of idealism, trust, and the work
he did at sculpting his CV around
this internship. Of course it could be worse;
he actually could've had less guile, been bound
to the promises he made his mentor.
He smiles remembering how she believed
his direction had that innocent torque,
but rudderless beings don't supersede
their teachers. He looks around, then decides
which of the judges has the weakest eyes.

29

Dumbed down

Then, stepping into her place was grotesque,
a Blair's witch project or a test of space
and garbage, how to weave through, how to get
from one point to the other in a daze
of flash realizations, clutter-thick
and strange as the Orient, imagined
Morocco with its thin claustrophobic
streets, its dangers. She'd already driven
around the airport circle seven times
while they stiffly followed in their rental.
Now their dumbed-down hearts wake up their numbed minds:
the years of slurred phone calls, the hints, and their
own complicity, her apoplexy
at such odd things, not so odd now, it seems.

High and dry

Shades of gray and a few splashes of mauve
fill the living room; with time his palette
has simplified along with his life, loads
of things have disappeared, though he doubts it
is anything but growth. The emptiness
of his rooms is not the same as caries,
those infinitesimal holes that blessed
his first profession. Now cosmetics please
him more, fab dentistry! What took two years
in braces he cures in two days. The art
could boggle your mind. He opens a beer.
All that's important is how good Denmark
makes beer, lifting his glass to single life.
He'll live fine without furniture and wife.

Perky

A perky attitude will take you far.
She smiles wide to teach the Home Depot clerk.
There's nothing about life that isn't our
own doing. It just takes a little work
to go where you want to go, or to be
where you are; her errands run, afternoon
mapped out for her, but first maybe she needs
to take a nap, nothing like a short snooze
to keep us on track; her husband won't be
home for a few days, his job is travel.
Oh, for goodness sakes, she might as well sleep
the day away. Her plans can wait until
a few hours before his plane arrives.
She'll shore up some happy dreams for the drive.

30

Thesis

He's awful happy fiction isn't life,
Madame Bovary didn't have a Visa,
Scarlett O'Hara's Tara Enterprise
didn't fund her race for mayor of Atlanta,
Anna Karenina got no Prozac,
the same not prescribed other heroines
whose new awakenings would lead to lack
of thesis subjects. Nice how they hem him
in years of study; thank God misery
finds good company in fiction's pages;
otherwise, he'd have to do surgery
or lawyering or clean monkey cages,
looking for odds and ends to please his mind.
Now he just need read of lives gone awry.

Antithesis

She couldn't stand at the train station without
dwelling on Anna's dive, or that story
about the librarian's horrid route
to subway death, Tolstoy's biography
or his final train ride to flee his wife
who was kept out as he died, war and peace
until his end. She wished she could stifle
all she knew when the train whistle blew, each
piece of fiction fired neurons forever.
Authors should be more careful what they write,
be responsible for what they tether
to the minds of readers; it is a blight
on literacy that so many lives
live in so many heads and *never* die.

Stasis

Before she could even open her book,
the cross-eyed cat was at her feet, purring
in anticipation. Before she'd look
for her glasses, the black one was lurking
and the fight for their roosts began, spoken
in tongues that needed little translation,
rough and tumbled speech high-pitched, rhythmic, in
striations that filched appreciation
for their affections, but short, decisive.
The black one took her lap, held high his head.
The cross-eyed one waited for her to lift
the cover of her tome then gently read
the scene, climbing up the back of the couch
to lie at her head. Winners all, no doubt.

31

For want of a wife

He'll become no geography, float free,
unhitched, unmoored, unburdened, smartened, he'd
flee now except for the slowed-down heart stream-
lined by live affection still. He's parried
the pain already. He needn't rush. Rest
would be refreshing after festooning
all those yellow ribbons for so long; nests
are made for robbing, so says the cuckoo –
or was that the cuckold? Oh hell! he'll do
now whatever he wants to do, no wart-
hog-tied marriage to stop him now. So few
go west these days. Let her go. He'll depart
as soon as he moves out of these doldrums.
Life must be more than this beat of humdrums.

Seeking efficiency

She caught him with dandelions sticking out
his mouth, his nose turned up at Kentucky
blue grass, crocuses, and freshly mulched ground.
He wanted what he wanted, rousting weeds,
taking them down neat, quick; wild things have no
manners but efficiency, no wasted
motion – as death should be. She had to know
which kind used the least resources to make
a decision. She'd seen a squirrel fresh
dead on the road; by her calculations
too much horsepower was used and gas, guessed
starvation was best for conservation.
She smiled to think of her affinity
to the groundhog and his efficiency.

Feeding fish

It was not want of money – she had means.
It was not for love of danger – she'd been
to Mexico, scared by the color scheme.
It was some driven thing in her, so thinned
by long life, shaved and matted down, mistakes
torn out of picture albums as if gone
when they were no longer there. For the sake
of her children she'd stayed alive, but long
ago she'd turned to dust, mere motes in air
floating on fate of breezes. They didn't see
her in the same way you breathe without care
just knowing air's there. No reason really.
She just up and walked into the ocean,
seagulls overhead, ospreys, pelicans.

32

Long marriage

She wrote his memoirs while he dictated
out of one side of his mouth. He didn't know
how she resembled St. Vincent Millay
stealing from him while they shared a pillow.
A chip on her shoulder, an ax to grind,
she told! deliberately misunderstood
his intentions which he had reminded
her of many times. It came to no good,
the whole affair, a huge mistake; regret
that he upset his wife will plague him now
more than the sheer pleasure of her young flesh –
or not? Remembering is a thrill somehow
unblemished by the bad publicity.
Nice you can give up but keep memory.

Marriage five

Husband four moved back to his neighborhood.
She wondered if you could call him husband
when the marriage was less than a year. Good
products had expiration dates, beer and
aspirin, for example, and she guessed
her elasticity should have one, too.
She'd concluded that last marriage had stretched
her well beyond her capacity, though
this fifth one has, too; she's counting the days
and the ways to tell him now that she knew
she would tattoo an expiration date
next time. It'll save heartache – money, too –
to insist on ink, not on wedding bands.
It may help, too, in finding the right man.

Long division

Out of another hazy sleep that kept
him in those thick Georgia mornings when doves
cooed in the green air and his mother wept
in the kitchen if the maid gave less love
than she thought was due her, those O'Neill days,
the long days' journeys to nights, when a boy
had no words for insanity, unswayed
by knowledge. Now his name pecks the unspoiled
dark and his mind barks and barks. He had thought
his last days would be filled like a loved one's –
beloveds bringing first violets sought
simply for his eyes, perhaps the last long
vision before indivisibility.
He didn't factor in disability.

33

Fever

She thought it peculiar the way this love
had curled around the edges, closing in
on itself like a fist she thought she'd gloved.
She couldn't understand how it could happen,
most terrible because she couldn't even
dislodge its momentum predicting it.
Now she is left to reverse this fever,
her hands tied by his cruel look of *nothing*
that sent her hope tumbling head over feet.
She trudged up the five stories dragging
the cartload of food as if she would eat,
faced the door as if she could imagine
life behind it. The stone cold aloneness
filled her like breath, drowning her in absence.

Toothache

So odd that a smart man who quotes Shakespeare,
who learns his lines like Houdini untied,
who knows exits and enters and endears
himself to clowns and royalty alike,
so odd that a man who can walk tightropes,
can juggle, play polo, read Kant, so odd
all that talent pools in just the one source
as if he were the low ground high skill sought,
odd how one and all know his brilliance, one
and all admire his so fine attributes,
one and all believe he can't be undone –
but if one night out of the blue, acute
pain comes, his strength is moot, it fades away,
toothaches very democratic that way.

Bellyache

If she were to answer you about it,
she would tell you they walked all cares away,
down trails with beaver dams, lady's-slippers,
how they got lost and used up a whole day
around a kettle pond Henry David
had mapped; it was sickening how green she
had become. If you ask her about it,
she's apt not to tell you, not to be mean –
but just like the burnt child who fears the flame,
her tongue rejects all recollections seared
in her heart from that time. She gave no name
to what they had had, only colors neared
the song they had made, starting belly deep,
inside, where now, only hunger keeps green.

Acknowledgements

Some or parts of the poems in this collection have originally appeared in the following publications:

◇ *Segue 2.2:* Soap Opera Sonnet 31

◇ *RI Roads:* "Providence" from Soap Opera Sonnet 26

◇ *The Newport Review:* Soap Opera Sonnet 17

◇ *The Providence Journal Bulletin:* "Her Kid's Been Around the Block" from Soap Opera Sonnet 4